nina campbell's
DECORATING
SECRETS

Nina Campbell

SHOPPING BAG SECRETS
SUE WEINER AND
FRAN MICHELMAN

nina campbell's

DECORATING SECRETS

Easy Ways to Achieve the Professional Look

text by helen chislett

special photography by jan baldwin

CIMA BOOKS
London

For the joy of colour

First published in Great Britain in 2000 by Cima Books Ltd
32 Great Sutton Street
London EC1V 0NB

10 9 8 7 6 5 4 3 2 1

A CIP catalogue record for this book is available from the British Library

ISBN 1 903116 08 2

Photography by Jan Baldwin
Designed by Janet James
Edited by Alison Wormleighton

Reproduction by Bantam Prospect, Essex
Printed and bound in Singapore by Tien Wah Press

Contents

Introduction

My third decorating book coincides with a time when so much has
changed in design. Detail and quality have become increasingly
important, not just to those lucky enough to have big budgets with
which to decorate, but to everybody who is passionate about how their
home looks. It has also become increasingly clear that there are
two paths people can choose to follow in terms of style: the Zen-like
interiors of minimalism or the more elaborate results of classic
English decorating. I do not have to spell out which side of the fence
I sit on: not everybody has the discipline to remain as purist as
many contemporary styles demand. When working with clients, I often
have to reuse some of their existing possessions because of either
budget or emotional attachment. That is not a bad thing – having to
incorporate certain items into a scheme can be the catalyst for a whole
set of creative ideas. This is one of the reasons why I hope that this
book will promote a desire in people to opt for ease and comfort over
rigid perfection.

As regards who this book is aimed at, the answer is simple: everybody. Many of my customers have been loyal to me for years, but I am always thrilled when the young like what I have to offer as well. I am also encouraged by the amount of people who enjoy using my wallpapers, fabrics, paints and carpets. These allow everyone to combine the Nina Campbell look with their own ideas and inspiration. Many people say that my ranges have kick-started them into updating something in their own homes, without feeling they have to alter the whole scheme. I consider that a compliment, and indeed this book is aimed just as much at those who want to adjust something minor as at those who are looking to decorate from scratch.

I particularly love it when people tell me that previous books of mine are now dog-eared and tatty from being referred to over and over again. I hope that this book, too, eventually develops a less than pristine state. You should find it an easy and enjoyable read – light-hearted, in fact – but with plenty of ideas that are absolutely sound when you pause to consider them. I hope it will encourage you to extend your own vision, rather than slavishly following what is shown. I want to instil the joy of decorating, not make people afraid of it. It has been enormous fun exploring my personal kit bag of decorating secrets and trying to put them into a cohesive format. Now I hope you find that they do indeed enhance your own life and home.

Nina Campbell

The Professional Approach

Many people can't understand why anyone should want or need a professional interior designer. It is automatically assumed that if you buy a home you must know what to do with it. Most people do have good ideas when it comes to, say, colours – it is, after all, an intensely personal choice – but often what they don't realize is the full extent of what else needs to be thought about when decorating a home.

All too often when decorating, people rush to the fun bit, like choosing paint colours and fabric swatches. But there is a whole layer of important decisions that must take place first, even though they may not play a major part in the way it looks. If a home is not practical, then it is not going to be comfortable and you will always be irritated by it. Function is key: imagine flying in from halfway across the globe and wanting nothing more than a hot shower and supper in front of the TV. Now think how frustrating it would be to find that the water is going to take several hours to heat up and you can't sit in your own drawing room comfortably with a tray on your lap.

Page 8 *One end of Nina's own drawing room.*
Nina made the doors larger to bring scale into the
room and create vistas through to her study.
Page 9 *Nina chose plain curtain fabric because it*
would not date so quickly or dominate a scheme.
You can add interest and colour through trims such
as the tassels and edging shown here.

You would probably end up wishing you weren't there, which would be a sad reflection on how well your home fulfils its primary function – to cocoon you from the world outside.

Begin by thinking about the layout of your home, the flow of space and the functions and requirements of each area; this should help you plan any plumbing or electrical work that needs to be done. There are security issues, for example – alarm systems are best installed early on if they are not going to be intrusive. Reliable and controllable heating is essential, but deciding where to position radiators can be a headache. You don't want to have a radiator where you were planning to have one glorious piece of furniture. Under-floor heating is one option, but in fact radiator covers are made in so many different styles and finishes these days that conventional radiators are often still the best option. Placing radiators under windows makes sense because they warm the cool air flowing in from outside. However, you might also want another one elsewhere in the room for when the curtains have to be drawn. Never sacrifice comfort to aesthetics – have as many radiators as you need but camouflage them well rather than trying to get by with scarcely any.

Lighting is also important. You should be able to walk into your home and flick a switch that controls all the lamps on a ring circuit, rather than walking from room to room switching on each one individually. If you don't sort this out from the beginning, the chances are you will end up sitting at one end of the drawing room

Above *In Nina's drawing room, she has used a magnificent William IV daybed to visually separate one seating area from the other. The beauty of a double-sided piece of furniture like this is that it can also be used to link the two ends of the room when she has more guests than usual.*

each evening because you can't be bothered to get up and switch the other lights on. Always install more power points than you think you need – at least two twins for each wall – so that you have the flexibility to move lamps around. And don't rely heavily on a central ceiling light; often it flattens and dulls a room, rather than bringing it to life as good lighting should do.

Don't feel locked into convention. If you are tall and have a small bath, consider changing the layout of the bathroom in order to have a generous-sized tub that you will really enjoy. If that can't be done, perhaps you should think about ripping the bath out completely and replacing it with the most invigorating and energising power shower imaginable.

Perhaps you know what you want to achieve, but don't necessarily have the money to put it all into practice. Don't despair. Making compromises is not always a bad thing; in fact, they can ignite some clever ideas. Try to draw up some sort of master plan showing what needs to be done first. It might be that you can afford to install professional lighting, for example, in which case it will make such a dramatic improvement to the room that it won't matter if you have to wait a few months for the upholstery fabric or curtains you have set your heart on. Alternatively, it might be best to buy the most inexpensive version of one thing in order to afford the expensive option of another – for example, to budget on the flooring and so allow sufficient money for one fabulous piece of furniture. The mistake would be to buy everything from the middle-price bracket, which will almost certainly not result in the effect you want. Your home is an extension of your own personality and it is this that you want to capture when putting your decorative scheme together.

Left *The sumptuous creamy curtains in Nina's bedroom, resplendent with tassels and tie-backs, would look perfectly at home in an English country house. In fact, the window looks out on a quiet London street.*
Right *For Nina, sensual ingredients such as flowers and scent are not luxuries, but essentials.*

Above This joyous toile de Jouy was the starting point in Nina's bedroom. The richness of the colour and the complexity of the design set the romantic and feminine tone. The bedhead, bedlinen, curtains and antique fringed bedspread have been kept plain as a foil to this – only the curtain fringing and frilled silk lampshades punctuate the neutrals (see inset right).

Finally, be prepared to edit some of your possessions in order to achieve the look you desire. Very often decorating is not so much about adding in the new, as taking out some of the old. I am not advocating the minimalist approach – anyone who knows my look would realize how alien that is to me – but rooms can grow tired if furniture, paintings and other objects remain static for too many years. Try to look with a fresh eye on your surroundings and keep your mind open to the many different possibilities a room offers.

Where to Begin

The first job of a would-be interior designer is to look at the basic shell of a room and consider all its potential. You have to train the eye, so that no matter how unpromising the existing decor is, you can look around and imagine everything stripped away, with only the skeleton remaining. A room may be crammed with hideous furniture, be painted in shrieking shades or have the sort of patterned carpet that makes you feel giddy, but you have to rise above this and see only the structure that lies underneath. There is a lot of work to be done before reaching a final decision, but simply by looking and studying, you can begin to germinate the first seeds of creativity.

For most people, the hardest part of decorating is combining function – the uses a room has – with the space available. The secret is to pay as much attention to unglamorous issues, such as storage, as you might to choosing a floor or curtain fabric.

Deciding
What You Want

Having assessed the canvas on which you are going to work, you must now think about the functions of the room. The idea is to end up with a space that works for you – not for the next person who might live here or those who might visit. Try to keep your mind as open as possible and to look beyond the room's obvious uses. In a living room, for example, you might ask yourself whether this is primarily a family room or one that has a more formal use; who uses it, including pets and guests; whether you are going to watch television here; whether the room is used mainly in the day or at night; whether it is used all-year round; and what activities take place here, including anything from playing the piano and reading to stamp-collecting and yoga.

Apply these questions to other rooms too. A kitchen is likely to be more than a place where food is cooked. It might also be used as an informal family sitting room with a TV and a sofa; it might be where the dogs sleep, where the children do their homework or where you wrestle with the family accounts. All these activities would have to be considered alongside the cooking ones. Similarly, a bathroom might double as a home gymnasium; a dining room as a study; or a spare bedroom as a sewing room.

Once you have drawn up a list showing who uses it and for what, begin to consider how the room breaks down into zones for various tasks. For example, you might like to vary the position of the chairs in the living room according to whether you are watching the television or entertaining friends. If so, you must allow some flexibility when furnishing. What is important is to use all the available space, rather than ending up a room where everything happens at only one end and every chair faces towards the television.

Left Your first task when designing a room is to think about how you want to use it – this cosy sitting room with the fireplace at its heart epitomizes tradition, comfort and a sense of well-being.

Overleaf A billiard table might not be a conventional piece of furniture, but if it is essential to your quality of life and you have a space where one would fit, then build the rest of the room around it.

Space and Style

Now that you have considered the functions of a room carefully, you can allow yourself to be led by other factors, such as the architectural style of your home. It is not that this should dictate how you decorate a room, rather that it should add another layer of inspiration.

The first thing to do when assessing the possibilities of a room is to study it from all angles. Consider the dimensions, noting the length of each wall and the ceiling height. Now look at the proportions of the room, including its shape and the height, width and position of doors and windows. Consider whether there is a natural focal point (for more about this, see page 30). Look at the architectural features – do skirting boards, picture rails, doors, a fireplace or other integral parts of the room suit its style? It could be that they have been added on at some later date. As you continue looking, you might also spot intrinsic problems the room has. It is rare to find a space that is perfect in every way; nearly always there are modifications to be made. Perhaps the ceiling is too low, the windows are too narrow, the door opens the wrong way or the natural light is poor.

The next step is to look at ways of solving some of these problems. Quite often, making doors wider and taller can add a greater sense of scale to a space. Perhaps there are structural alterations that would help – knocking through to an adjacent space, removing bulky fitted cupboards, introducing a cornice of some description. If these decisions are beyond your budget, don't despair – decorating a room well can mask many of its faults.

Think about the views into a particular space and also what you see from it, such as the view from one room into another. A hallway, for example, offers glimpses into adjoining rooms – these should look as inviting as possible, enticing you to enter the home. A simple thing, such as keeping a doorway open, can create quite a different ambience. Walk around the room you are planning to decorate, thinking about the traffic routes from one area to another and what you would see from each point. Don't just concentrate on the obvious views – those from the windows and doors – but think about what else you would notice walking in for the first time. Remember to take into account eye levels when sitting as well as when standing, so that there is something to catch the eye at all times. You can distract attention from ugly or awkward corners by highlighting the beauty of something else.

CHECKLIST

- Who will be using this room and what will they use it for?
- How suitable is it for these functions at present?
- Are any structural alterations needed? (This might not be major work such as knocking down a wall – it might be widening a door or taking down a picture rail.)
- Is there any plumbing or electrical work to be done?
- Does the architectural style detract from or add to the overall ambience?
- How does the room relate to those around it?
- What are the views like, both from inside to outside and through internal doorways?
- What are the room's best features and how could these be accentuated?
- What are its faults and are there any obvious solutions?
- Can you 'see' in your mind's eye how you would like the room to look?
- How are you going to allocate the budget you are working within?

Right *Accentuate the strong points of your house – the eye is led through this elegant hall by the direction of the floor and the sweep of the stairs. An arched doorway adds extra interest.*

As much as possible, try to cultivate your eye so that it can look beyond the perimeters of a room and take into account the total space available. Don't misunderstand me – I have not suddenly become an advocate of one-space living – but what is important is to be aware not just of the room you are working on, but also how it relates to the surrounding rooms.

Homes should have a thread running through them, linking each space with the next. It jars the nerves if there is too much of a jump aesthetically from one space to another. You don't have to repeat schemes, but rather try to pick out themes within them that can be carried through to the next room. A carpet, for example, can set the standard for the range of colours to be used around it; or you might take the colours from one room and use them in a different configuration in the next. The idea is to achieve a balance and harmony that make the ambience of a home really special and comfortable. You don't want anything within it that jostles for attention or detracts from the feeling of calm you enjoy there.

Left *You can create some wonderful effects not only with light but with shadow too. These rattan blinds filter the light, so that the whole room takes on a much softer and more atmospheric look.*

Right *If you have connecting doors from one room into another, you must plan carefully what will be seen from each side. Try to make a link through colours or flooring.*

position other pieces around the centrepiece in such a way that nothing detracts from its overall effect. Give it space, so that the eye will rest on it as you enter the room.

Depending on what it is, you should then consider whether your anchor piece needs dressing in any way; should it be specially lit perhaps or be given a different background colour? Try walking from room to room in your own home and noticing where your eye falls as you enter. Now try to think of ways of enhancing that effect.

Focal points are not only about having a big, important piece. It is also fun to have smaller tableaux that you enjoy once you are sitting down and relaxing. A collection of small objects, for example, can draw attention when displayed well at sitting height. Or you might want to create a theatrical effect by displaying a collection of plates, hats or some other three-dimensional item on one of the walls. The idea is to create a delightful effect, so that the eye is stimulated wherever it pauses.

If you are decorating from scratch, you have a big advantage: you can find an object you love and use it to hold the rest of the scheme together. Take inspiration from its shape, colour and texture and use these as a basis for key decorating decisions. It is much easier to work this way round than to decorate a room and then begin the search for the one perfect centrepiece.

CHECKLIST

- Is there an existing feature that would make an eye-catching focal point?
- How could it be dressed up to look really special?
- Do you have an idea for something else you would like to introduce?
- What are the maximum dimensions of such a piece?
- Would the room benefit from having more than one focal point?
- Where would you like the eye to fall when entering the room, when sitting in the room and when moving about it?
- Could lighting and colour be enhanced to help the overall effect?
- Does your chosen focal point offer inspiration for the rest of the scheme?

Left The fireplace is the natural focal point of most rooms, but you can accentuate its importance through mirrors, fire tools and mantel ornaments.

Right An antique gilt mirror suits the grandeur of the wallpaper in this drawing room. The marble-topped console table below emphasizes its ornate quality.

Using Pattern and Colour

This is the part that everyone loves, but that also causes the biggest headaches. Not only can it be disappointing to find that the fabric swatch you ordered with such optimism does not look quite as you intended, but it is also an expensive mistake if you get it wrong. Professional decorators make up 'storyboards' for clients showing swatches of paints, papers and fabrics, but it takes an experienced eye to know what these will look like when used.

The problem is understanding both light and scale. The blue that you love in a tiny swatch might be oppressive once it is covering all four walls of your dining room. The vibrant tartan you so admire might have a startling effect once you see it used to cover a large piece of furniture. That is why it is always worth buying a roll of wallpaper, a good-sized fabric swatch or a sample pot of paint before making your final decision. Before investing a large amount of money, try living with these things – move the samples around the room according to what time of day it is and how the light falls. Always try to buy items that go together, so that you build up a complete look; this helps enormously when you move into a new home.

Let us think about colour first. Forget about what the decorating magazines say is in or out of fashion. Look around your own home and gather together some of the things you love. Open your wardrobe and pull out your favourite shoes, scarves or jackets. Raid your make-up bag for favourite eye and lip shades. What was the last decorative item you bought? It might have been anything from a teapot to a bedspread, but take a fresh look at it and see whether the colours relate to the other things you have looked at.

Left *Fabrics such as this glorious upholstery cloth are a satisfying way of introducing colour, pattern and texture into a decorative scheme.*

The point is that over the years we all build up our own colour palette that we feel comfortable with and enjoy. It makes sense to use this as the basis for decorating our homes. That is not to say you should not be open to other possibilities – it is in finding base colours that are easy to use and then layering them with more dynamic shades.

Don't fall into the trap of worrying over what goes with what. In truth you can mix any colour with any other; what matters is the intensity of the colours you choose. A fierce Mediterranean blue will not look at its best teamed with a washed-out sage green, but put the same green with a denim shade of blue and it harmonizes beautifully. Colour fashions come and go, which is why I have evolved ranges over the years that are guaranteed to complement each other whether they were launched last year or ten years ago. There are other ways of reflecting design trends in a room without overdosing on colour.

Often I advise clients to keep walls and curtain fabric relatively plain – that way they know they are guaranteed many years of use from them. Curtain trims,

Above left Views are an important consideration when decorating – not just the one you can see through the window, but the tableau you create on a side table too.

Above In a large room, it makes sense to keep walls and windows fairly neutral and to introduce pattern and colour through the more transient elements: upholstery, cushions, lampshades and accessories.

CHECKLIST

- Make a storyboard using magazine cuttings, decorating swatches and anything else inspirational.
- Now try to relate that to the room you wish to decorate, considering light, proportions and other factors.
- Decide on the base colour – the one used in largest quantities.
- Think about the other key ingredients – windows, upholstery, flooring.
- Try to create a neutral scheme into which colour and pattern can be introduced.
- Order samples of wallpaper, paint and fabrics. Cover a large square MDF board with each of these, so you can move them around the room.

upholstery fabrics, rugs, cushions covers and lampshades are a much more flexible way of introducing bold colour into a room. They also encourage people to be braver than they might have intended, because small patches of colour are not going to have the migraine-inducing effect that whole walls might have.

The same goes for pattern. There is no rule book that says you cannot mix florals with stripes, or checks with paisleys. The key is in not having too much of each one and being careful to have a little space between them. Pattern brings vigour and excitement into a scheme, so don't be frightened of introducing it. But if you are cautious, then opt for a set of cushion covers to begin with, rather than reupholstering everything.

Finally, if you fall in love with a fabric that would look wonderful but would really cut too deep a hole into the budget, think about using it in smaller amounts – to upholster a favourite chair perhaps, or even a cushion, rather than make an expansive pair of curtains.

Small Space Living

Before anyone accuses me of giving advice that is only relevant to those with grand houses and big budgets, let me introduce you to my son Max's home. Nothing could be more ordinary than this small, terraced house in London, the typical choice of a first-time buyer. Like most sons, Max was not keen on his mother taking over his first independent home – he has strong design ideas of his own – but I was allowed to give him a certain amount of guidance.

Above *By blocking off a doorway, Nina made room for this full-size sofa. Tortoiseshell lamps provide a glamorous touch.*

Left *The wooden shutters at the window not only provide privacy from a London street, but strike a contemporary note in Max's comfortably laid-back sitting room.*

Many of the points already mentioned have relevance here. In a modest house such as this it is even more important to make the space work for you. Originally the sitting room was two small but separate rooms, each with their own doorway. They had already been knocked through, but both doors had been left in place. Simply by bricking up the first, we immediately created enough wall space for a decent-sized sofa. We then introduced a second fireplace at the other end so that the room achieved more balance.

Linking the outside to the inside makes sense in any house, but particularly in one short of space. Making a garden door from the sitting room was another improvement because it gave the impression of space flowing from one area to the next. Colours were kept very neutral, with shutters at the window for privacy from the street outside. Careful budgeting allowed Max to spend money on the things he wanted to – such as a state-of-the-art sound system.

One thing that is essential to small space living is to think about storage requirements. It is all too easy for a house like this to look cluttered and chaotic. We built floor-to-ceiling shelves wherever we could, not only for books and photographs, but for clothes and shoes too. The golden rule here is that whatever you possess must have a home within your home – and that you must be disciplined enough to put things away.

Left *At the other end of Max's sitting room, Nina made a doorway out into the garden, which accentuates the airy feeling. There is a fireplace at each end of the room, giving a sense of proportion to the space.*

Another important consideration is flow: how adjacent spaces relate to each other. In a small house, it would be jarring to go from one strong colour scheme into another. Here we created a feeling of harmony throughout the house, which also had the effect of making the rooms appear larger than they really are. It is good to have an awareness of how other rooms look as you walk through your home. By keeping the carpet the same and the colours neutral, a more unified look was created.

Once Max's own possessions were brought in, the room took on his own character: it could hardly be described as a typical Nina Campbell room, which was just what he wanted to avoid. This is the important thing when decorating – take

Above *Deep curtain headings add to the scale of the room by emphasizing the proportions of the windows. These ones are formal without being feminine.*

Right *In a small house, storage is all-important. Floor-to-ceiling shelves were built in wherever possible to house Max's ever-increasing number of books as well as personal mementoes.*

Above *Simplicity is the key when decorating a modest-sized house. This applies not only to colour schemes and window treatments but also to less obvious considerations – such as how the bed is dressed or the flowers arranged.*

Right *Colour schemes can be continued right through to the smallest detail in a room.*

advice and look for ideas by all means, but don't try to emulate the exact look you
have seen elsewhere. It is your own pictures, books, personal treasures and keepsakes
that mark out your home from everyone else's. And don't think that just because you
do not live in the house of your dreams, professional decorating tips are not relevant:
as Max would testify, it helps to make sense of a space through clear thinking before
adding in colours and furnishings.

Above *A walk-in closet with
generous storage is a wonderful asset
in a house like this – it means the
bedroom can remain the calming,
tranquil space it should be.*

Right *Max's bathroom picks up the
same colour palette as the bedroom,
which is perfect for the rustic-looking
tongue-and-groove cabinets, simple
fittings and shuttered windows.*

The Decoration

Now that you have a good grasp of what a decorator does, it is time to apply what you know to an individual room. The fun starts here: fabrics, papers, paints, carpets and all manner of accessories can be combined to produce the look you want. The trick is not to think about these things in isolation, but to consider how each ingredient works with the others to build up a look that is both visually stunning and absolutely practical. Think of a room as having many layers, each of which needs to play its part in the overall effect, from the large elements, such as sofas and windows, to the smallest candle shade and cushion.

The next few chapters are devoted to specific rooms, from the hallway to the bathroom, and are designed to inspire you further when decorating your own home. The advice applies whether you are putting together an entire scheme from scratch or looking for ways to give your existing decor a rejuvenating facelift.

Halls

The most important fact to keep in mind when decorating a hall is that it is a room in its own right. At times there is a resistance to this idea: people think of a hall or landing as a through-route to other more important rooms and so they rarely spend the same time, energy or money on the decoration. But a hall is pivotal, not only because it provides the first impression of your house, but also because it sets the tone of what is to come. Doors leading off from a central passageway give tantalizing glimpses into other rooms.

Left *Scale and grandeur have been introduced into this narrow townhouse hall through the classic marble floor, elegant stair runner and marbleized dado.*

Above If you are lucky enough to have
a large hall, it is a good idea to
incorporate some kind of sitting area
into it – the ideal place in which to read
the papers or open the mail. Here a
fireplace makes a natural focal point
around which chairs can be arranged.

Right Impressive doorways have the
effect of blurring the boundaries
between hall and drawing room. To
counter this, the black outline of the
inlaid marble floor delineates where one
space stops and another begins. Slim
black borders mark out the other areas.

Adjacent Spaces

Although the hall must be considered as an independent area, it is also important to
think about the rooms adjacent to it. This is particularly true if doors are often kept
open, because you do not want a jarring effect as the eye is led from one space into
another. The same is true of stairs – these are a bridge between the upstairs and
downstairs not only physically but also aesthetically. There should not be too much
of a visual leap as you move around the house.

Floors are an excellent way of emphasizing where one room stops and another
begins. Hard floors – usually wood or stone – are ideal in halls, as they can
withstand a lot of wear and tear, whereas carpet is the preferred choice in most
drawing rooms. Changing the floor while keeping colours and wall decoration similar
is an ideal way of linking one room to the next.

Making an Impact

If you are lucky enough to have a large hall, it can be the ideal place in which to display your most treasured possessions – be they paintings, oriental rugs, fine pieces of furniture or one grand pièce de résistance, as with the magnificent vase shown here. In other words, a hall offers the opportunity to create your own private gallery. It is also the perfect setting in which to create pockets of interest and excitement: a chance to whet the visual appetite of guests.

Although halls are primarily through-routes to the rest of the house, they can be enjoyable places to sit, so if you have room, include a sofa or chairs – as is usual in the country. Even in a modest-sized hall, you can achieve a similar effect. It helps enormously if you can resist the temptation to use the hall as a dumping ground for various pieces of household flotsam – coats, shoes, dog leads, umbrellas, bicycles or buggies, for example. If you don't have a large cupboard where such essential but unattractive items can be stored, then you should think seriously about having one built. The hall should be a calming, serene space – a tranquil atmosphere where you can mentally catch your breath on entering the house.

You may be tempted to choose a bolder than usual colour for your hall, and certainly this can create an immediate impact. But you do have to consider how it will blend with the rooms around it. It is not wise to choose adjacent colours that vibrate too strongly, as you want friends to feel soothed on entering your home. Good lighting is also important – it should not be so bright that it makes visitors blink after coming in from the darkness outside, but neither should it be so low that they run the risk of tripping on the carpet edge. It should give a warm and welcoming feel in the winter and in the evening, and a calming atmosphere in the summer and in daylight. Once you have achieved the perfect canvas on which to work, introduce much-loved furniture and objects that convey the message you want to send about your house.

Left *The sumptuous malachite vase in this grand hall has been given an even greater sense of importance through the addition of a mahogany-and-gilt base.*

Improving Proportions

Don't despair if your own hall is flawed in some way – too small, too narrow, too low, too dark. It is possible not only to camouflage such imperfections through clever decorating, but even to make features of them. If you need convincing, take a closer look at the room shown on the right. As with so many spaces, it had good points and bad. The good was the lovely domed skylight, which flooded the hall with light. The bad was the fact that, incredibly, the windows only came up to neck height. It was very disconcerting not being able to look out of them, so I decided to dress them as if they ran from floor-to-ceiling, tricking the eye into thinking the proportions were correct. It was simple enough to do: by covering the wall with a striped blind hung from normal window height to where this window began and hanging a pair of heavy taffeta dress curtains at each window, the illusion was complete. Not only did it hide the ugliness of the windows, but it drew the eye upwards towards the skylight, which I then accentuated with a beautiful cut crystal and ormolu dish light.

Above *The caramel-coloured lacquered finish chosen for this dark lobby makes an eye-catching backdrop for a collection of decorative medallions.*

Right *The tops of these windows only come to the bottom edges of the blinds, but the window treatment cleverly gives the impression of height and proportion.*

The Total Approach

Before making any major decorating decisions, consider carefully who is going to use this room, what they are going to use it for and when they are most likely to be in here. You might have a drawing room that is used far more in the summer than the winter, for instance, or in the evening as opposed to the day. It might have many functions, perhaps serving as a place in which you entertain guests, write letters or escape from the children to read a book or newspaper. It could have less obvious uses, too: maybe you meditate or play the cello here, or use it to display your best-loved paintings or objects. All these activities should guide you when planning the layout of the room.

You must also assess the strengths and weaknesses of the room in terms of proportion, architecture and permanent features. If this is a space you plan to use mainly by day, it is important to study the natural light and consider ways of boosting it if necessary. If it is linked to another room – the dining room perhaps – you must consider the view you will create from one room into the next. Entrances are fundamental to the success of a room.

The drawing room shown on the left links first to a library and then to a dining room. It was important that each room had its own identity while retaining a visual connection to the others, so I took the palette of apricots, greens and blues and used it in different combinations to keep a sense of harmony. If the room has a fault, it is that it is rather low. The two huge mirrors at each side of the fireplace help to rectify this by bringing scale into the room and extending the view. The candelabra in front of the mirrors accentuate this and create something really dazzling, so that for a moment you cannot work out where one space ends and another begins. It is a magical effect.

Left Floor-to-ceiling mirrors at each side of the fireplace have the effect of tricking the eye into perceiving the room as taller than it is. They also draw the eye into adjoining rooms.

Left Silk damask walls were the starting point for this grand scheme. Gilt mirrors emphasize their richness. *Right* Marquetry and ormolu continue the palatial theme – this handsome chiffonier has been dressed to spectacular effect.

Once any flaws have been masked, you can concentrate on bringing in layers of decoration to achieve a really glorious effect. A beautiful patterned carpet, elegant wallpaper or magnificent curtain fabric might be the starting point from which you work. Don't despair if you can't afford all three: buy well for one and it will make a world of difference. Then raid the rest of your home for the finest pieces of furniture or the best paintings you have – it is amazing what people often have tucked away down a dark hall or in a guest bedroom. Think of your drawing room as the room that is always open to the public and you can see how important it is to put the best you have on display.

Seating Areas

Because drawing and sitting rooms fulfil many uses, it is important they are laid out with some flexibility. The most depressing sight is to walk into a drawing room where the sofa and chairs are arranged in a U-shape around the television. As a general rule, it is best to put the TV somewhere else in the house altogether, but if this is not possible, at least try not to draw such obvious attention to it.

Although houses should always be primarily designed with the owners in mind, you should also allow for entertaining – we are social animals, and sharing meals with friends and family plays its part in our overall quality of life. When you think about it, it makes no sense to have a dining room that seats twelve people comfortably if you can seat only six in the living room. Try to avoid the problem by having more seating easily available – fender seats, for example, are an excellent

Left *A sofa and two armchairs provide the main seating area around the fireplace in this drawing room with walls covered in creamy damask.*

Above *At the far end of the room is a second seating area around the window, with a table where cards can be played. It is easy to marry the two together when extra guests arrive.*

Left If you have a lovely view into a garden, position a chair near the window or door so that you can enjoy it to the full.

Below left Window seats are an excellent way of using up corners of space, and they come into their own when you have additional guests.

way of providing seating for an extra couple of people, as are window seats. You might also plan to have two sitting areas in a room: a more intimate one around the fire for family or a small group of friends; and a separate one – perhaps near a window and arranged around a table – that can be used for playing games, studying or reading the newspapers. This way, when you find yourself with more guests than usual, you can seat everyone comfortably just by moving some of the key pieces of furniture around. The joy of having a carpet over a woodblock floor is that if you love giving parties – as I do – you can just roll back the carpet and you have the perfect dance floor.

Try to put yourself in the shoes of someone walking into your home for the first time. Stand at the door of the drawing room and look in: does it look inviting enough that you would immediately know where to sit? The most unwelcoming rooms are the ones where you feel as though you are sitting in someone's particular chair. The

Left *A seating area must also have an appropriately sized table – this one was chosen bcause its slim proportions echo the dimensions of the room.*

Right *The gold and ruby damask of this elegant occasional chair makes the perfect companion to extravagant stripes and sunshine yellow under-curtains.*

celebrated interior designer Elsie de Wolfe advised that you should never have one chair stuck out on a limb as invariably someone rather shy will sit on it and then feel too embarrassed to move closer to everyone else. Now sit down and look around. If you were to offer your guest a drink, would it be obvious where he or she could put it down? There is little point having enough chairs if you don't have surfaces within easy reaching distance of them. And if those surfaces mark easily, it is up to you to protect them in some way – your guest might well be thinking of other things.

The aim is to induce a feeling of well-being. Make sure the drawing room is heated sufficiently and is fitted with sympathetic lighting – when friends come in from the cold outside, they want to feel warm and protected. This is another reason why you should make a point of using your own drawing room on a regular basis; rooms that are not regularly heated and ventilated soon develop a rather austere and intimidating atmosphere. When people leave for their own homes, you want them to be thinking only of what a wonderful time they have had.

Left *Red is a colour that many people shy away from using, but it gives a room immediate warmth and vibrancy.*

Above *The upholstery colour has been reflected in the curtains. Scallops and loops of fringing draw the eye upwards.*

Above right *Curtain fabric has been twisted into rosette-shaped tie-backs, which emphasize the extravagance of the window treatment.*

Comfort Above All

The one thing that I demand from a drawing room is comfort. It makes no sense at all to lavish time and money on a room if it results in an effect so grand that guests perch upright on the edge of a sofa, too nervous to put a cup down on a table. The drawing room might be the place in which you present your public face, but that does not have to be a scowl – it should be a welcoming smile.

A really cosy armchair in which you can lie back with your feet on a stool is not a luxury but an essential. Don't we all long to kick off our shoes and flop on a familiar chair at the end of a stressful day? For that reason you mustn't choose furniture for shape or style alone – try it out first, so that you can be sure it will eventually mould to the contours of your own body. Ideally, you should have a combination of soft and hard-backed seating. Anyone who has suffered backache will know that deep, squashy sofas are not always the kindest. Guests should be able to find a place to sit that will help them feel most at ease.

However, creating a feeling of comfort is not just about buying good-quality seating – it can be suggested through decoration, particularly fabrics. Curtains and upholstery fabrics bring softness, a sense of being cocooned, into a room. This subliminal message can be accentuated through the colours, patterns and types of fabric you choose. Silk, for example, remains popular not only for its luxurious look but also because it has such a tactile quality. The same is true of many other choices – chenille, velvet, linen, crewelwork and voile. The role of trimmings, such as tassels, fringing, ribbon or braid, is to add another layer of luxury. It doesn't just please the eye, but makes us feel pampered and therefore relaxed.

Cushions are essential because they have the effect of making seating look even more inviting. However, they should not be arranged so stiffly that guests feel too inhibited to rearrange them. As with everything else in the room, they should have both a visual and a practical use.

Right Neutral walls and creamy fabric make the perfect foil for the rosy boldness of the upholstery design, complemented by the richly decorated cushions.
Left A rust-coloured, chunky trim around a plain cushion gives it more resonance within the scheme.

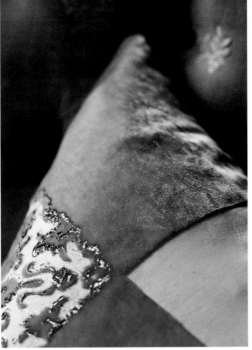

Building the Look

A successful decorating scheme brings together many ingredients to form a cohesive whole. If you are not planning on using a professional decorator, you must train your eye to think about the details as well as the big picture.

Always err on the side of simplicity. There is much to be said for using neutrals as a basis for a scheme, because it then allows you to bring colour in through upholstery fabrics, cushions, rugs, lamps, pictures or flowers. These are far more versatile than wallpaper or carpet. Drawing rooms in particular lend themselves to neutrals, but they should be 'happy' neutrals – not cold colours which have a depressing effect. Neutral drawing rooms also contrast well with dining rooms, which are a more obvious place in which to use strong colours. Introducing themes and colours onto a neutral canvas has another advantage: it makes it much easier to subtly alter a room from winter to summer or day to evening, to ring the changes according to your mood.

This approach makes accessorizing even more important – everything from the tie-backs you choose to the depth of bullion fringing on the sofa will play a part in building up the final look. It is also probably the most enjoyable part of decorating, the icing on the cake.

Left *The calm, serene atmosphere in this London drawing room was achieved using a harmony of greens and neutrals. The close-ups reveal how the smallest details played a part in the finished scheme.*

Having seen a room through from the beginning, you can be overtaken by a sense of elation towards the end. However, it is important to retain a sense of discipline. It is all too easy to become distracted by the beauty of a trimming or tassel, but you must keep focused on the key colours you have chosen to work with and the overall look you wish to achieve.

It might be that you have designed a room around a particular theme, such as the dinner service shown in the dining area on the right, which is at one end of the drawing room shown on the previous spread. This can be doubly rewarding when a room is finished: you have created a beautiful space and in addition have made a backdrop for something you love. Collections such as this not only bring a decorative element into the room, but provide inspiration for colour, pattern and texture. They also give the room a stamp of personality and originality.

These last two ingredients are essential if you are to end up with a room that will give you satisfaction and happiness. By all means take inspiration from images around you, be they in magazines or books like this one, but don't forget the golden rule: you are your own client and you want a room that is unique to you, rather than a replica of someone else's home. Your signature should be apparent in every aspect of your house.

Right The dining area at the other end of the drawing room shown on the previous spread uses the same colour palette, but achieves a different character through pattern and furniture.

Dining Rooms

Your dining room is a theatre: the place in which you weave a little magic to entertain and entrance your guests. You may use it for formal lunches, most probably at weekends, but it is more likely a predominantly nocturnal space – and lighting, colours and textures have to be chosen with this in mind. You also have to think about how the dining room links to adjacent rooms: by day you may want to screen it off entirely, but when entertaining friends at night it is wonderful to allow tantalizing glimpses of a beautifully laid table and shimmering candles. Even the most jaded of your guests will be encouraged to rise to the occasion if the room – and therefore the food and wine – looks inviting enough. The scene is now set for a memorable and stimulating evening.

__Right__ The midnight blue of the damask-lined walls gives this dining room a nocturnal flavour. However, it was also important to link it visually with the adjoining suite of rooms.

Far left The dining room gives the illusion of being lit by candles alone. In fact, it is illuminated through concealed spotlights, some of which are positioned to highlight paintings.
Left A custom-made breakfront cabinet provides storage space for everything from silver and glasses to linen and candlesticks.

Creating a Mood

It is essential in a dining room to maintain an illusion of perfection, even if it is a false one. You may use the room rarely, but this should not be apparent. Untidy corners where children's homework has been thrown aside, tarnished silver or dusty surfaces will detract from the magic. Your guests should feel pampered when they walk in – after all, the care you take over dressing your dining room says as much about how you feel about them as about yourself.

Consider first how well your dining room works from a functional point of view. How is food kept warm between the kitchen and the table? Do you have a generous area in which to serve? Where is food put between courses? Is there enough storage for silver, china, glasses and linen? The only things that should be on view are those you are using.

Lighting is the next factor. There is quite simply nothing to beat candlelight in a dining room because it is so flattering – to you, your guests and the room itself. However, you also need another source of low-level lighting so that guests can see what is on their plate and where to find the mustard pot. If you are carving or serving food from the sideboard, this needs to be well lit so that there are no mishaps with a knife and you can see what you are serving.

Left *Golden trim on the curtains picks out the yellow of the under-curtains, which allow light to pour into the room by day.*

Below *Tassels and tie-backs in the same colours emphasize the feeling of abundance within the room.*

The room should have easily controlled heating, too. Walking into a cold dining room is not conducive to good cheer – but after some food and wine are consumed, temperatures tend to rise, so an over-warm room can be equally uncomfortable.

Once these practical issues have been thought out, you can then concentrate on the decorative ones. Colours, curtains, table accessories, paintings and mirrors are the tools with which you create your stage.

Left *The gilt mirrors double as candelabra and are guaranteed to create a brilliant night-time effect.*

The Dedicated Dining Room

The trend is to live in smaller and smaller spaces, so the dining room is often squeezed out to become a home office or extra bedroom. This is a shame because it is rather wonderful to have a room set aside for entertaining, whether it is Sunday lunch for the family or a dinner party for friends. Eating, talking and laughing with people cements friendships and is integral to our well-being as social creatures. Informal suppers in the kitchen or intimate soirées in the conservatory have their own appeal, but if you are lucky enough to have a dedicated dining room, hang onto it: for one thing it looks likely that the pendulum will soon swing back in the dining room's favour.

This is in part because it makes sense from a practical point of view. Dining areas in other rooms tend to become submerged in everyday clutter, so there is a great deal of tidying up to do before the cooking even begins. The whole process of entertaining runs so much more smoothly when there is a separate room in which all the paraphernalia of dining is kept, from dinner services and wine glasses to candelabra and soup tureens.

Having a room set aside to dine in also means that you can push the boundaries out a little when decorating. After all, this is a room in which you want to create visual impact and which is seen mostly at night: put these factors together and you realize you can be braver than usual. Colours can be stronger, wall decoration bolder, ceilings more visible, furniture more ornate. Dining areas in other rooms have to conform to what is already in place, but separate dining rooms can have a different atmosphere. Their role is to create a small jolt of delight when guests walk in for the first time.

Right The elaborate trompe l'oeil design on the walls and ceiling of this Hong Kong dining room masks unsightly air-conditioning panels and service doors. There is a play on what is real and what is not.
Above left The room is a harmony of East and West, juxtaposing traditional Chinese paintings and European-inspired furniture.

Above *A change of table setting can transform a dining room from day to night, winter to summer. Here, Brussels lace and Derby plates create a delightful, Bacchanalian mood.*

Above right *Place names in delicate silver holders ensure that your guests feel welcome while silver and lace ensure the table enhances an evening's atmosphere.*

Dressing It Up

The focal point of any dining room is, of course, the table. How well you dress the table makes the difference between a moderately pleasant meal and an unforgettably elegant one.

Think first about the table itself. If you own a beautiful one, then show it off: there is no need to cover it with a cloth unless you are anxious to protect it. If you like to vary the look, then one simple rule is to use a cloth for lunch parties and leave it uncovered at night – that way you can enjoy the reflection of candlelight on the polished surface. If your dining table is not attractive, however, don't despair. Once it is covered with a beautiful damask or linen cloth, no one would know whether it is Georgian mahogany or an MDF sheet.

Consider carefully how many dining chairs to buy. You may entertain ten people on average but if you do have space for fourteen around the table, it makes sense to have fourteen chairs for those rare occasions you need them.

There is a saying, 'You can never be too rich or too thin' – and to this I would add, 'or have enough tableware'. For example, you do not have to buy glasses only because a couple have been broken and need replacing: you could buy them simply for their glorious colour or intriguing shape. The same goes for place mats, napkins, plates, flatware, serving dishes and coffee cups. As any chef will admit, ninety

per cent of the success of a meal lies in its presentation. Think how you could show off your favourite dishes to best advantage by presenting them in a more imaginative way – or turn this idea on its head by planning what dishes you might make to suit the set of plates you are longing to buy.

Formal table settings will always look fabulous, but you can bend the rules a little to suit your budget. You could, for example, begin collecting glasses of one particular colour, such as cranberry, but from many different sources. You could even mix antique with modern; with the colour to unify the look, it would still be a success visually. What is important is that everything you use is maintained to a high standard: there must be no smudges on glasses or smears on silver. Always allow enough time when entertaining to check each item carefully.

Carry the colour theme you have chosen through to flowers, candles and place settings. There does need to be a central display of some sort. A simple arrangement of flowers and fruit is ideal for lunch parties, while a more contrived display gives a sense of occasion to a more formal evening meal. Make sure that this is either low enough or tall enough that guests can still see each other across the table. Be careful how you position candles, too – setting fire to the table centrepiece is an over-dramatic way of starting conversation.

Left *Flowers are one of the most effective and immediate ways of dressing a table – take inspiration from their shape, scent and colour.*

Right *This magnificent silver stand, with its romantic, pastoral theme, makes a splendid centrepiece for flowers or fruit.*

Versatile Dining Rooms

In a modest-sized home, a dedicated dining room may seem too much of a luxury. Rather than sacrificing it entirely, you might be able to find ways of utilizing the space better so that you get more than one use from the room.

In my own London house, the dining room is in the basement adjacent to the kitchen. I have rarely had a formal dining room; my previous one doubled as a billiards room and this is a dining hall. It also serves as the library, which works well on three levels. In the first place, I have, like most people, an ever-increasing amount of books, and this is an ideal space in which to store them from floor to ceiling. Also, books are an effective way of bringing colour into a naturally dark room. Thirdly, they provide a great talking point at the beginning of an evening.

The room is versatile in other ways too. The centrepiece is the table designed by David Linley. It seats eight comfortably, but has an additional top which extends the capacity to fourteen. I can either leave it uncovered to make the most of the beautifully polished surface or cover it when I want to create a more intimate mood. Although I entertain here mainly at night, I do use it for occasional lunch parties too. This means that lighting is very important: there is not enough natural light, so spotlights on the ceiling boost this during the day. At night, lights on tracks around the edge of the room wash down over the books, creating a dramatic effect. The deep, rich colours are not ones that people think of using in dark rooms, but, in fact, it makes more sense to go with

Left *Nina's own dining room doubles as a library for her extensive collection of books. The table, designed by David Linley, can extend from seating eight to fourteen.*

Above *The smaller the detail, the more effective it can be. Personalized calligraphy on a bay leaf is an enchanting touch.*

the flow rather than kick against it. Intense colours like these create a fabulous night-time atmosphere.

One thing I am passionate about is storage. This underpins good design because without it any room will look a mess, no matter how beautifully decorated it might be. The wall opposite the window in my dining room is decorated with beautiful

hand-painted panels which conceal deep floor-to-ceiling cupboards, filled with plates, glasses, vases, serving dishes and all the other essentials of elegant dining. The panels blend into the book-lined walls, so that at first glance they seem to be purely a decorative addition, rather than a practical one.

One thing I had to sacrifice in order to create this feeling of being wrapped within a wealth of rich colours was the fireplace. It was of no practical use within the room and took up far too much space. Don't be afraid to take similarly drastic measures to achieve

the look you want. On the whole, architectural features are a boon, but they should not interfere with how well a space works on a practical level.

It goes without saying that, for me, one of the joys of entertaining is dressing the table. Each layer – plates, glasses, napkins, flatware, flowers – is chosen both for its individual beauty and how it vibrates visually with what is next to it. Not that table decoration is a substitute for stimulating conversation or witty repartee: the people gathered around the table are the most important ingredients for a successful evening. However, if you take care to set the scene properly, they will play their part with ease and enjoyment.

Above Pockets of colour-coordinated food, like these rosy nectarines, bring another layer of interest to a table.

Right The table is covered for evening use with a Moroccan silk bedspread which brings out the richness of the amethyst walls. Painted panels conceal storage.

Kitchen Dining

One of the most refreshing changes in the way we live now is that entertaining no longer necessarily means a formal dinner in the dining room. For many people, the kitchen is the hub of the household – the place where food is both prepared and enjoyed. It makes sense to eat breakfast or lunch here, but don't overlook it as a setting for evening entertaining, too. You might not be able to fit so many guests around the kitchen table, but having space for four or six means you can still create an intimate supper-party atmosphere. If you are preparing the food yourself, it is much more enjoyable to have people to talk to while you work, although this kind of occasion can be so casual that it is best suited to evenings with close friends rather than business associates or new acquaintances.

Right The fresh green and blue colour scheme in Nina's kitchen was inspired by her collection of plates.

Studies and Libraries

A study does not necessarily mean a place in which to read and work – the word can be used to describe a small sitting room, often a more cosy area than the more formal drawing room. There is something peaceful about places like this, so it is no wonder that people often think of them in terms of retreats for the men of the household. Your first decision when decorating one is to think about who will use it most and what they will use it for – reading, sewing, doing homework, watching television or pursuing a hobby of some sort. Libraries, on the other hand, have a very specific use: the storage and enjoyment of books. Sometimes the two are combined in one room, but often they are entirely separate.

Left *Nina's study is more a cosy family sitting room than a place to work. She chose dark woods and red tones because it is used more at night than by day. Interestingly, the panelling and fireplace are, in fact, a faux mahogany paint effect.*

Private Passions

In many households, the study is still the man's domain: a sanctuary from the hurly-burly of family life. In many ways this is fair enough – after all, most women rule the roost where the rest of the home is concerned. All of us are entitled to a corner we can call our own and one of the pleasures of having a study is that it offers privacy and a space in which to pursue our own interests.

If the study is not to double as a family sitting room, the chances are that it will acquire a very masculine look, since a good-sized desk, a robust chair and ample bookshelves are the essential requirements. It can also be the perfect place in which to display and study collections. These might well provide the starting point for your scheme. Think about where items are best displayed in terms of height, choose a background colour that will show them to best advantage and light them well. Collections are a wonderful way of bringing character and colour into a room – a number of similar objects grouped together has ten times the visual impact that an individual one has, no matter how beautiful it might be. Items that can be wall-mounted are an excellent alternative to paintings.

Above and right *The colours and lighting in this city study were designed as a backdrop for a collection of Napoleonic soldiers.*

Far right *Panels of false books slide back to reveal a state-of-the-art music system. The television and video recorder are concealed in the same way.*

Overleaf *Two Chinese vases filled with glorious red roses look wonderful against the citrus green of the walls.*

The Masculine Touch

There is a type of look for a study that is synonymous with English style and tradition: think dark-panelled walls, a marble fireplace, book-lined shelves and sturdy furniture. It is a style so classic that it will simply never date – decorating trends come and go, but the gentleman's study endures. It is replicated around the world from here to Hong Kong, as with the one on this page.

Not everyone has the space for such a room, and certainly you do need generous proportions in which to recreate this look properly. One challenge today is combining a style that has been around for a hundred years or more with modern technology. This sort of study is not likely to be chosen by someone running a business from home, but is more likely to be a secondary workplace or the control room from which the rest of the household is run. However, computers, phones, fax machines and televisions are often essential requirements for modern living. More often than not, a music system will also be required. The secret is to install a wall of storage, which at first glance looks as if it only houses books. Have it custom-made to conceal all manner of unsightly wires and equipment – cupboard doors or false books can then

Left *This traditional panelled gentleman's library is actually in Hong Kong, although it has a quintessentially English look.*
Below left *The Buddha by the window and the view overlooking the harbour indicate the true location of the room.*
Below *This classic book-lined study has a wall of cupboards behind which the fax machine and other technology are concealed.*

open out to reveal what lies behind. Specialist paint techniques have become so sophisticated over the past few years that it will be possible to make it look as though it has been in the room for decades.

Sombre colours and pools of soft light are part of this decorating approach. However, you can introduce pattern through curtains or upholstery, with which to punctuate the dark surroundings. Books and other publications inject interest, as do favourite paintings, photographs and other personal possessions.

Although the desk is probably central to the room – the focal point, in effect – it is important to include an inviting seating area as well. After all, other members of the family might want to talk in here, or to sit and read or listen to music. If you have ever been to a gentleman's club in London, you will know the sort of atmosphere that typifies this style of study: dignified and restrained, but also superbly comfortable.

Bedrooms

Your bedroom is the most personal room within your home. It should offer you sanctuary from the day's cares — an oasis of calm in which you can feel rejuvenated and soothed. Bedrooms are much more than places in which to sleep. The most successful ones have a bed-sitting room quality, which means they can be used for all manner of things — from writing letters or having facials to burying yourself in a really good book, confident you won't be disturbed. If you design your bedroom with this in mind, you realize that it is just as important to create the right atmosphere for daytime use as it is for the night. Allow yourself to feel indulged here and you will find it far easier to cope with whatever worries life throws at you.

Left Warm neutrals have been used here to create a restful retreat. Classic stripes throw attention onto the bed, while cord has been used to give definition to the room.

Right, far right and below right

Attention to detailing is what matters when building up a cohesive look like this. Everything, from the butterfly lampshade to the curtain heading and cushion fabric, has been chosen to work in the scheme as a whole.

If you have space for a small sitting area in the bedroom, then apply the same rules as you would to a conventional sitting room: chairs should be comfortably upholstered, with surfaces at hand for cups or books. Rather than settle for fabrics that echo those of the bed, choose ones that have slightly different patterns or tones, to help mark out one area from the other. It is also lovely to have space for personal mementoes, especially family photographs or much-loved paintings.

Consider when you are most likely to use such a cosy sitting room. Many women long for somewhere private to which they can escape occasionally during the course of a day – perhaps to read the newspaper, make telephone calls or write letters. But if the bedroom enjoys a pleasant aspect, it might even be somewhere you could invite friends to have a morning coffee (assuming the rest of the bedroom is absolutely pristine, of course). Conversely, it might be an intimate corner in which you and your partner can catch up with each other's day, or the place your children gravitate to when there is something they want to tell you.

Opposite *This generously proportioned bedroom, also shown on the previous spread, has been laid out to include an intimate sitting-room corner. The cushions on the sofa match those on the bed, making a visual link between the two.*

The key to creating a bedroom where you feel removed from life's cares is to make sure you are surrounded by the things you consider essential to quality of life. If you love to read in bed, for example, it makes sense to have floor-to-ceiling shelves at each side of the bed filled with much-loved books. You must also have a well-positioned light to read by. If this is the place you like to indulge yourself with face creams or manicures, then a well-positioned dressing table is a priority.

The bed itself must be superbly comfortable, but it should also look inviting and seductive. Fine-quality bedlinen is not a frivolous buy, but the kind of luxury that, once bought, you wonder how you ever managed without. A headboard that supports the back comfortably when you sit up in bed is also a must. Bedrooms are, above all, sensuous places, so indulge yourself as much as possible whether it is with flowers, scented candles or fine fabrics.

Below left *If you do not have a private bathroom or dressing room, it is essential to mark off a section of the bedroom for your personal use. Dressing tables are not only excellent as storage but are recognizable female territory.*

Right *Bedrooms should appeal to the senses, so make sure yours has an element of indulgence. The simplest arrangement of freshly picked flowers is a delight both in terms of colour and scent.*

The Well-Dressed Bedroom

For many people, a four-poster bed is the height of elegance and romance. When you climb into one, it feels as if you are on an island, or perhaps a boat that will transport you to another world. However, if you are planning to have one, remember that it must be done well or not at all. Four-posters use vast quantities of fabric – not just on the curtains around the sides, but also on the ceiling canopy, both inside and out. The effect is sumptuous and regal, so it must never appear to have involved penny-pinching decisions. Don't be deterred if your bedroom has fairly modest proportions and a ceiling of only average height – it is possible to buy such beds custom-made, and they will make a room appear larger than it is, rather than smaller. That is because they trick the eye, making you subconsciously believe that it must be a large bedroom to fit in such a bed.

You also need to think carefully about the backdrop you are going to give such a strong focal point. Plain walls are fine for a contemporary look, but glorious beds demand a more decorative setting. A large, floral English chintz is ideal, particularly if it provides a visual link to the bed drapes through either pattern or colour. Pattern is a wonderful design ingredient, which, happily, is making a comeback, and bedrooms are the perfect place in which to use pattern because it injects a feeling of warmth and

Right This English country house bedroom is, in fact, in an apartment in Hong Kong. Ceilings are low, but fitting in a four-poster bed and chandelier has the effect of making the room appear better proportioned than it really is. The chintz is a heavenly design by Jean Munro.

cosiness. However, it is important to offset it with plains as well; the eye will become tired if the effect is too riotous. This is one of the reasons why dado rails are so effective – they provide a visual break and the opportunity to introduce a plain area adjacent to a patterned one. They are also one of the most immediate ways of giving a modern apartment, like the one shown here, a classic look.

Once you have embraced the formal, classical style, you must continue it through to the rest of the furniture within the room. Think about symmetry: a pair of tables or chests with lamps flanking the bed is both practical and aesthetically pleasing. It endures because it looks right. However, you could opt for a chest on one side and a table on the other, so long as they are of the same height, allowing

Above The far end of this guest bedroom, also shown on the previous page, has room for drawing-room style furniture to make those staying here feel truly at home.

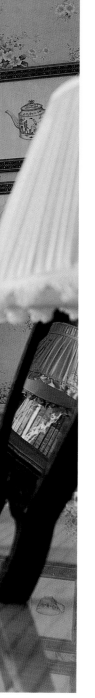

Right *Bedrooms allow you to be more adventurous with pattern than in other rooms. Here, black-framed etchings give an anchor to the scheme.*

Below *The delightful Chinese figures of a husband and wife strike a harmonious oriental note in this guest bedroom.*

the lamps – which must match – to be in line. If you have room, a piece of furniture at the foot of the bed – a chaise perhaps or a stool – will emphasize the feeling of grandeur, as well as providing a convenient surface on which to rest a breakfast tray or put the bedspread.

If you want to achieve a feeling of elegance, try to introduce pieces of furniture that would be as at home in the drawing room as in the bedroom. A bookcase or writing bureau will look as fitting as a dressing table or wardrobe, and will help the bedroom double as an extra sitting room by day. There should also be somewhere comfortable to sit, particularly if you are lucky enough to have a lovely view to enjoy. Window seats can be a boon. Lamps, pictures and books give a homely feeling, which is important if you want to avoid ending up with a bedroom that would look better suited to a hotel than a house. Classic style should always be combined with comfort, and prettiness with practicality.

Above *Adjustable reading lamps within the canopy of the bed are not only decorative but kind on the eyes, too.*

Lavishly Layered

The decorated look is the antidote to minimalism. It requires the designer to introduce layer upon layer into a room, building up a look that appears to have been in place for ever. To achieve the decorated look yourself, you must be committed to following it through down to every detail. So many people hold back at the end, ending up with something rather half-hearted and therefore disappointing.

First you must find your starting point. For me, this is usually a fabric because it is through colour and pattern that I set the style of the room; the luxurious quality of soft furnishings is pivotal to the success of a scheme. If there is a matching wallpaper available, so much the better. Using one bold pattern for walls, windows and upholstery is a way of bringing an immediate signature into a room, giving it character and interest. Think of it as the diva of your scheme, while other, coordinating fabrics are the equivalent of the chorus.

Be lavish with whatever material you choose. Better to use reams of something inexpensive than to cut corners with the fabric you long to use. Perhaps you can't afford to make curtains with your number one choice, but could use it to upholster a stool instead. Try not to be led by fashion too much when making your decision. This is a look that transcends current fads and is designed to withstand the passing of time. Think of English country houses with bedrooms that have not changed for many years — the idea is to create something equally enduring in your own home. Coordinating fabrics add another layer of interest to the look. Stripes, trellises or sprigs are ideal choices, as they add variety without being overwhelming. Think too about the colour of linings; a glimpse of another colour can be tantalizing to the eye.

Right *This half-tester bed sumptuously dressed in auricula-inspired chintz and elegant stripes evokes the atmosphere of a French château. In fact, the bed is in a city penthouse.*

Left *To give more scale to a modest-sized bedroom, the curtains have been hung right to the ceiling. Vertical stripes also help to trick the eye into perceiving the room as being taller. The dressing table was custom-made to fit the tiny space available.*

Private Spaces

Your bedroom is not just a treasured sanctuary but also the place where you prepare the face you present to the world. This means having space in which to pamper yourself – a private corner that is yours alone.

For most women, this is the dressing table. It need not be a conventional design: writing bureaux, side tables and chests-of-drawers can be commandeered for use if necessary. The essentials are a good-sized mirror and a generous surface on which to keep beauty products. Ideally, it should be placed near a window, but artificial lighting is also necessary to boost dull mornings or for use by night. A chair or stool of the appropriate height is also advisable, but if space is tight you could push this against a wall when not in use.

Good storage is the key to keeping bedrooms calm and serene. This applies not only to clothes, but to each individual area within the room. Dressing tables should never be allowed to get dusty and messy because that is no way to start a fresh day. Drawers are a boon for tucking unsightly or bulky products out of sight, but you should also think about the way other items are stored. Make-up brushes, for example, need to be kept upright and clean; cotton balls and cotton buds require containers of the appropriate scale.

Devise different ways of giving yourself a lift each morning; for example, a simple vase of flowers on the dressing table is lovely to focus on when you wake up. However, the most important thing is to make clear to other members of the family that this is your own domain – not an additional surface on which they can throw down keys, spare change or old receipts. Men do need the equivalent of a dressing table surface if they are to respect this. It need not be in the bedroom: if you have a separate dressing room or en suite bathroom, it might be better to give them a private corner of their own in there.

Bedside tables should be kept as free from the flotsam and jetsam of daily life as possible. Choose the largest you have room for, so that you have space for a lamp. Smaller lights positioned over the headboard are ideal for reading by. You also need room for essentials such as books, reading glasses, a clock, water and a telephone. Flowers are a lovely additional touch and you will appreciate their scent as you sit in bed. You should always be able to control lighting from the comfort of your own bed, and to have at hand all the things you might require through the night.

Right Fine bedlinen is a way of introducing a note of luxury into the smallest of rooms. The painted bedside chest echoes the colours in the dressing table (see previous page).

Left *Hidden doors are witty and fun. This one is camouflaged by false books concealing the entrance to the bathroom.*
Right *The dark beams of this London guest room set the tone for the colour of the wallpaper. Shutters let in light while blocking out unsightly views.*

Guest Rooms

There is more to having people to stay than simply providing a bed for the night. You want guests to leave your home feeling relaxed and well looked after, warmly anticipating their next visit. A lot of this will depend on the room itself. Often, guest rooms double as something else – a home office or hobby room, perhaps. This might be essential given the size of your house, but when other people come to stay, it should be *their* home too. That means any other activities that take place here should be tucked well out of sight. Utilize built-in cupboards, the space under the bed, high shelves or chests – it doesn't matter what form the storage takes, so long as there is enough of it. It is simply not fair to expect guests to negotiate an exercise bike, artist's easel or computer workstation in order to get into bed.

The next consideration is how much storage you have provided for your guests' use: not just space in which to hang or fold clothes, but an area for shoes, luggage and the like. People need to unpack in order to feel properly comfortable, and it is disheartening for them to open each drawer and find it already full to bursting point. There must also be a dressing table of some sort, a large mirror and at least one extra chair on which clothes can be hung overnight.

Finally, bring in as many homely touches as possible: books, magazines, photographs, flowers, drinking glasses and bottles of mineral water.

Integrating Storage

Achieving harmony between function and aesthetics is the secret to a successful

bedroom. Having enough clothes storage is a primary consideration because without

that you will always find yourself living in chaos. If clothes are bulging from your

existing cupboards, spend an afternoon sorting out your wardrobe. Put all your

clothes, shoes and accessories into three piles: things you never wear, things you

rarely wear and things wear a lot. The first category probably consists of items that

no longer fit or are out of fashion, so be disciplined and give them to a charity shop.

The second pile might include seasonal items or sportswear, and these can be

stored elsewhere in the house, as they don't need to be immediately accessible.

You should now have plenty of room for the third pile – the things you actually use. Now spend a couple of hours organising these into easily accessible colour-coordinated sections.

Built-in cupboards are often far too useful to discard on aesthetic grounds, but they can look so solid that they induce a feeling of claustrophobia within a room. Perhaps there are ways you could soften their impact – either through a decorative paint technique or by replacing door panels with stretchers of fabric. You could even cover the whole of the doors in fabric, to integrate them completely with the rest of the room, as shown here.

Opposite *The sliding doors of these fitted cupboards have been covered in the same fabric as the rest of the room, softening their effect.*

Opposite below and below *The summery voile at the windows matches the walls, but grey-blue curtains with heavy tassels provide a balance to its frivolous character.*

Dressing Rooms

If you have the space to create one, a dressing room is a great boon, as it allows you to remove all the paraphernalia associated with clothes out of the bedroom. By doing this, you create quite a different atmosphere within the bedroom: it is much more likely to become the calm oasis you long for. The dressing room, by contrast, is a busy place devoted solely to function. It is the equivalent of the utility room adjacent to the kitchen.

A dressing room requires very little except adequate clothes storage, good lighting, a generous-sized mirror and a chair. However, you must keep it tidy and well ordered. When designing your own, take a hard look at the clothes you need to store and work out exactly how much hanging and folding space you need. Cubbyholes for bags, shoes and belts are also an asset. Don't forget to allow for awkwardly shaped items, such as large hats or boots. Some kind of labelling system might also be advisable. If you have an impressively large shoe collection, for example, all stored within their boxes, take Polaroids of each one and glue them to

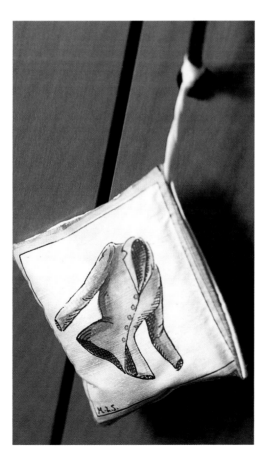

Far left A dressmaker's dummy provides the perfect storage place for ties in the dressing room which adjoins the bedroom shown on the previous page.
Left Illustrated labels are an amusing way of showing what is behind closed cupboard doors.

the boxes. This way you won't waste time rummaging through them all trying to find the right pair.

Make it a rule not only to put things away after use, but to check their condition first. Loose buttons, worn heels or stains need attending to at once if your dressing room is to run efficiently. There are few things more frustrating than taking clothes out of the wardrobe only to find you cannot wear them.

Left *This extravagantly draped dressing table is at one end of a small dressing room. Scallops of lace add romance.*

Right *The floor-to-ceiling cupboards have been painted with garlands of flowers to break up the solidity of the surface and reinforce the feminine atmosphere.*

Built-in furniture makes sense in a dressing room, not only because it makes maximum use of available space but also because it is likely to be custom-made to your own requirements. The interior should offer a comprehensive range of pull-out drawers, adjustable rails, hooks and shoe racks. Bear in mind that shallow drawers are easiest to keep tidy, but that you will also need deep pockets of space for luggage and the like.

A chair of some sort is essential in a dressing room — both as somewhere to drape clothes before putting them on or hanging them up and as a place to sit when trying on clothes or putting on shoes. You might also like to include a dressing table, telephone or ironing board.

Bathrooms

Bathrooms are the most intimate rooms of the house, the spaces where we can relish being alone. For many people, they are more than places to bathe – often, they are a retreat from the rest of the home. Bathrooms that are separate from the other rooms will have quite a different character to those linked directly to a bedroom, where you have to consider the flow from one area into the next. Decorative decisions are second to functional ones when designing a bathroom: the priority is to create a warm, safe haven with the best plumbing imaginable. Whether you opt for hard flooring or carpet, for tiles or for paint, plays second-fiddle to getting these other essentials right.

Left *Nina's own bathroom has been hung with images of her children, giving it a feeling of intimacy.*

Above Nina's bathroom adjoins her dressing room, where stacks of crisp linen and linen spray are a testimony to her organized nature.

Above right and below Glass-and-mirror shelving recessed into the wall above the bath provides the perfect place for Nina's favourite luxuries.

Opposite Nina redesigned the bathroom from scratch, which allowed the bathtub to be placed centrally. The panelling is, in fact, new.

In my own bathroom (shown on these pages and the previous spread), I wanted to achieve a look that is best described as classic with a twist. Sterile white tiles do not have the same appeal for me as rich, warm colours. I wanted a bathroom that had the ambience of a sitting room, rather than that of a hospital.

The faux tortoiseshell wallpaper is one of my own designs, and when combined with crackle-glazed wood panels, it makes me feel as though I am standing in an ivory and tortoiseshell box. The floor is solid oak – a material that many people assume is not suitable in the bathroom. In fact, when varnished properly, it is able to withstand water very well. I certainly prefer it to soggy carpet.

Having chosen very elegant materials and traditional colours, I wanted to emphasize the fact that this is a *room* as much as a bathroom. Introducing architectural features, such as the dado and cornice, was an important step towards this. However, my final touch was to cover the walls with pictures – mainly of my three children – but using sepia images, black-and-white prints and portraits, all of which are in keeping with an overall style. On the other side of the bathroom is my dressing room, which has deep built-in cupboards. The depth of these allowed me to design recessed shelving above the bathtub for assorted jars and bottles. The mirrored back accentuates the feeling of glamour.

Streamlined Sophistication

Many people desire bathrooms that are much harder-edged than the rest of the house. Materials such as marble are popular because they are durable to water and steam, while imprinting a signature of luxury onto a room. However, a bathroom that is covered totally in any hard, reflective surface, be it marble, another type of stone or tiles, often looks rather cool and austere.

Instead, think about combining materials that each bring different qualities to an interior. Wood and stone, for example, work well together: wood introduces a mellow, warm tone, while stone defines the contours of a space.

Because the bathroom is primarily a functional room, it lends itself to built-in furniture in much the same way as the kitchen does. Unsightly items can be kept neatly out of sight. Such furniture should follow the shape of the room as much as possible, so that there are no ugly gaps or sharp edges. Basins that are inset into the worktop also follow this precept and are both practical and aesthetically pleasing.

Right *The black-edged border of the marble floor reflects the contours of the work surface, bringing order to an imperfect space.*

Below *A small amount of black has been used to anchor the warm, neutral scheme. Introducing a dado is a way of breaking up wall space.*

Classic Cool

If starting from scratch, it is always best to choose white bathroom fixtures – other colours are too subject to the whims of fashion. However, that does not mean you should keep to neutrals throughout: floors, walls and built-in furniture give the perfect opportunity for stimulating the eye through both colour and texture.

Hard floors are still many people's preferred option for the bathroom because, in an area devoted to water, they are thought of as more hygienic. However, if the result is too masculine for your own taste, look for ways of softening it slightly – perhaps through windows treatments or by introducing a piece of furniture more usually found in a bedroom or sitting room. This will offset the more clinical elements in the room and provide a visual bridge from the bathroom to the bedroom.

Above *Brightly checked fabric picks out the blue on the walls and makes a cheerful focal point.*

Right *Using wood prevents this bathroom from looking too clinical, while chintz blurs the harder edges.*

Sensual Softness

Increasing numbers of people prefer to decorate their bathrooms much as they would other rooms of the house. That means fabrics, free-standing furniture, paintings and ornaments. Naturally, practicalities have to be tackled first: for example, steam is a destructive element, so you must have good ventilation in place. However, once that has been achieved, there is no reason why you should hold back.

Lighting, too, must be considered, not just on a functional level but in terms of the ambience it creates. Spotlights or wall lamps with dimmer switches are an ideal way of controlling lighting, allowing you to set the mood you require.

The joy of bathrooms such as this is that they express the owner's personality. The focus is not so much on the bath itself as on the decorative ideas and items that surround it. This approach also promotes the idea of indulgence, which is a seductive notion in the bathroom. These are not rooms to hurry through between waking and dressing, but rooms in which to unwind and soothe away the anxieties of the day.

Left *This elegantly shaped tub is the perfect antidote to the boxed-in look, and the fabric above the panelling creates a gentle background for it. Oriental paintings and figures give the bathroom a personal flavour.*
Right *Bathroom lighting need not be harsh – here, it has a softness appropriate to the fabric gathered onto the walls.*

Finishing Touches

Not all rooms require a complete overhaul. Many of them can be given a lift simply by editing some things out, repositioning others and introducing a few new buys. It is amazing how different a room can look with a new rug, a different set of cushion covers, a change of lampshades or better-hung pictures. Accessories and flowers also help newly decorated rooms become truly finished, so don't forget about them once the major items are in place. It is worth spending some time making sure that all the detailing is correct.

Sometimes I encourage clients to walk around their homes removing treasures from one room in order to dress another. A fresh location can draw attention to something that has been rather neglected in the past few years. However, it is also worth putting aside a slice of the budget for accessories that will inject new life into a room. If you love shopping as much as I do, this chapter is for you.

Above Nina favours layers of white-
and-cream embroidered cushions
and pillows in her own bedroom.
Left A sage-green chenille cushion
with matching throw brings out the
green of the upholstery fabric.

Above right When upholstery is
plain, it makes sense to match
cushion fabric to that of the curtains.
Right A mixture of patterned
and plain cushions offers the most
flexibility within a scheme.

Cushions and Throws

Cushions are an indispensable part of any decorative scheme, not just because they are essential to comfort but also because they introduce contrasting colour and pattern to a scheme. Altering the scale or design of a cushion can breathe new life into armchairs or sofas, while their soft plumpness is a very sensual ingredient. Pillows too offer much more than support for the head; piled up on a bed, they induce a feeling of well-being and luxury. Throws, often coupled with cushions, are a way of layering up softness and drawing the eye away from slightly lived-in upholstery fabrics.

Above Rather than choosing cushions that match upholstery, introduce those that vibrate visually with other colours. If upholstery is plain, you can be bolder with pattern.

Right Introduce texture to cushions through quilting or appliqué. Here, scalloped edges emphasize the femininity of the room.

Above Cushions are an excellent way of introducing patches of colour that might be too dominant in large quantities. This chocolate brown cushion is the equivalent of visual punctuation between soft lilac and green and the sugar pink in the foreground.

Tassels, Tie-backs and Trimmings

The importance of trimmings is often overlooked, perhaps because they seem expensive for what they are. However, they are worth their weight in gold because they give a scheme a truly professional edge – the equivalent of making sure a sentence is properly punctuated. They also offer the opportunity to make a room unique. There is such a wealth of sizes, colours and designs to choose from that it is doubtful you will see the one you choose used in the same way elsewhere. Curtain tie-backs are not only functional, but add an additional visual lift to the overall look of window treatments; narrow bindings in a contrasting colour on the leading edge and base of a curtain can define the line and give it a couture look.

Left An exquisite cut-velvet design in apricots and blues has been used to cover a French chair.

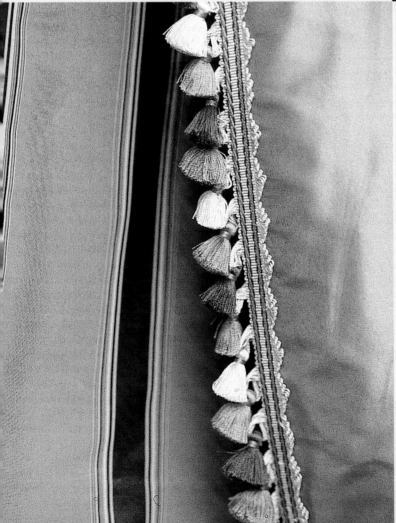

Above far left Heavily tasselled grey-green bullion fringing on the bottom of a sofa accentuates the richness of the scheme and echoes the grey-green in the carpet.

Above left There are myriad curtain tie-backs to choose from – these classically crafted ones pick up the colours of the curtain fabric beautifully.

Far left Nina often uses cord to define the edges of a room. It emphasizes the proportions of a space.

Centre left A simple window treatment is to make tie-backs from the same fabric as the curtains. This one has been enhanced with a matching rosette.

Left A blue-and-brown striped taffeta blind (shade) has been hung behind a pair of elegantly trimmed taffeta curtains.

Window
Treatments

Beautifully dressed windows will never go out of date because they are often the focal point of a room. It is not enough to choose a wonderful fabric: you must also spend time considering the heading, lining colours, whether to hang curtains from a track or a pole and which materials you favour for it; whether or not you require tie-backs of some description; and whether the curtains are for use or for dress only. There are so many styles of window treatment to choose from that it is always advisable to keep tear-sheets from design magazines if you see the look you want.

Above *An over-scale ruched heading slotted onto a pole is an eye-catching way of finishing off curtains, and it gives the impression that the window is taller than it actually is.*
Right *This shaped lambrequin has been designed to hide unsightly window fittings as well as having a decorative purpose.*

Above A wooden curtain pole with trompe l'oeil tassel finials has been coloured to match the curtain fabric and wallpaper.

Below An extravagant French-pleat pelmet with fringing and knotted cord detailing makes a bold statement.

Right A gilded bracket with shell shape has been used as a centrepiece for this sumptuous window.

Below right Austrian blinds (shades) are perfect for modest-sized windows where you still want to make a decorative splash.

Floors and Walls

These are the largest surfaces in a room, so what you put on them will determine the overall style. Try to introduce patterns which will give a room direction without swamping it. In terms of floors, that applies both to carpets and hard flooring, but pay particular attention to the borders around the edge of a room. For walls, you will have to choose combinations of paper, fabric or paint.

Top left A combination of hard floor and carpet is a practical solution when you want both comfort and durability. The dark border of this leopard-print design defines the boundaries of the room.

Above left Bathrooms offer the perfect opportunity to be bold with wall colour. Here, cream woodwork breaks up the vibrant green and black of the walls.

Above Many people automatically opt for plains when buying carpet, but a softly coloured patterned one, like this specially coloured Braquenie design, brings another layer of interest to a room.

Top right Painted garlands of summery flowers reflect the shape of the curtain heading and soften the appearance of solid cupboard doors.

Above right Large, geometric patterns impose order and scale. Here Nina's Pembroke wallpaper gives a sense of importance to a simple townhouse staircase.

Left Collections need not be confined to the decorative – even the way you set out glasses on a tray can make a strong aesthetic statement.

Displaying Collections

Collections bring immediate interest and character into a room. They are also expressive of your personality because often they are linked to your interests, the places you have travelled or to something in your family's history. However, they can be used simply to make a decorative statement: one piece of coloured glass tends to be rather unprepossessing, but a group makes a bold, visual statement. Consider where to position a collection so that it can be enjoyed to best advantage. Usually this means placing it at eye level – but bear in mind that this could mean eye level from sitting height. Keep a collection of objects together; there is no point diluting their impact by separating them. And always make sure they are immaculately maintained.

Above left *A collection of silver makes a dazzling display, with lamps at each side enhancing the effect.*
Far left *The simplest objects take on new importance when displayed as a group – here antique silver-topped champagne bottles form an interesting still life.*
Left *Personal treasures collected over many years stamp personality upon a room.*
Right *The mirrored back of this chinoiserie cabinet accentuates the impact of glassware grouped en masse.*

Left Bronze tribesmen on horseback look stunning against the graphically shaped bottom edge of a carved mirror frame. The modern vase makes an interesting juxtaposition.
Below left Monkeys and palm sconces set an exotic tone in a hallway, with an Indian feather headdress from the Amazon placed centre stage.

Above right This beautifully depicted soldier is part of a collection of Capodimonte porcelain military figures.
Right Antique match-strikers are a particular favourite of Nina's, being both decorative and functional.
Far right An enchanting amethyst crystal pug on a marble base sits on Nina's desk.

Objets d'Art

Superficially, these are the frivolous buys, the objects with no function except to delight the eye. However, that is function enough. Without these injections of personality, a room will look very dull indeed. Don't feel guilty about treating yourself to something with no obvious use; very often it becomes more treasured with time, rather than less so. In fact, many people find that items like this outlive the decorative scheme itself. It is through *objets d'art* that you remember the stories of your life – because an item is, perhaps, something that was passed down to you from another member of the family, a treasure you bought on holiday or a present from a friend on the birth of a child.

Wall Display

Many people have paintings or prints with which to decorate their walls, yet so often they pay little attention to displaying them really well. As with collections, the golden rule is to group them wherever possible. Vertical arrangements can be particularly effective. Good lighting is also crucial: if you want to enjoy a fine painting, it makes no sense to hang it in semi-darkness.

Above Consider scale when hanging a painting. This fine oil landscape has been complemented by a table of equally generous proportions.

Right Position pictures above pieces of furniture to which you wish to draw the eye.

Above far right The symmetry of this arrangement, with the mirror placed centrally between rows of vertically arranged pictures, reflected in the positioning of furniture.

Far right Nina designed this carved gilt frame in which to display a Derby dessert service.

Dressing the Table

One of the joys of entertaining is making the table look absolutely wonderful. When you lead your guests into the dining room, you want them to react with delight. Try to build up sets of china and glasses, so that you can vary your table settings a little. Investing in new table linen is one of the simplest ways of ringing the changes. It is also advisable to introduce a theme so that the whole look hangs together – it could be a witty visual link to the occasion you are celebrating or simply a colour. This could be picked out not only in linen and china, but also in glasses or carefully positioned vases of flowers. You should also think of ways of stimulating the senses: not just through sight and taste, but through scent, too.

Above *Perfectly folded jewel-coloured table linen gives an immediate lift to a scheme.*
Left *Sparkling glassware in appropriate sizes is an asset to any table.*
Right *A purple-and-gold cloth is the backdrop for Nina's Wedgwood plates.*
Far right *Blue glassware and red roses combine for a delightful table setting.*

Left Antique amethyst glass with silver leaf detailing brings a contemporary twist to the most elegant of tables. Choose one bold colour to collect and you can have enormous enjoyment adding to it over the years.

Below Sage and raspberry Limoges coffee cups have a Florentine feel which is very appealing. Mix and match the saucers according to mood. The gold rim and handles set the other shades off to perfection.

Above far left Bring in a breath of summer with two-tone tulip bowls in pistachio and strawberry. The colours are reversible so you can mix and match at will. Fine gold edging completes the look.

Above left Toile de Jouy blue-and-white cutlery is irresistible to those who embrace decoration with a passion. Think of the fun building up a table setting inspired by these knives and forks.

Far left Nautical themes are a perennial favourite, and these Directoire coffee cups with ship motifs are a must-have for those who love the sea. Their elegant shapes and soft colours are a delight.

Left Beaded rattan place mats are a wonderful addition to the home, not least because of the delightful shadows they cast. Available in a glorious range of colours, they give new meaning to the idea of trimmings and braids.

Flowers

The final addition, but by no means the least important one, is a flower arrangement of some description. Flowers have a truly magical effect upon a room – it is not just that they bring in a patch of brilliant colour often combined with enchanting scent, but that they bring life into a space. Whether you favour formal arrangements over informal ones, country blooms over the hothouse variety or house plants over cut flowers is entirely a personal choice. The important thing is to display them well in an attractive container and to look after them – just as fresh flowers strike a joyous note in a room, so wilting ones make a home look sad and unloved.

Above Orchids are delightful in an arrangement, not only because of their sculptural shapes and vibrant colours, but also because of the heady scent they release into a room.
Left The fragile beauty of an opening rose is hard to beat – roses are the quickest way of bringing the feeling of summer into a house.

Above Choosing containers for flowers is as important as which flowers you buy. The metallic sheen of this vase contrasts wonderfully with the distressed surface of the mirror and the matt of the stone fireplace.

Left Look for vases that have a touch of wit. Here, simple glass tubes spell out the word 'love', accentuating the romance of single stem roses.

Left The metallic wallpaper is Altare,
colour 2, from the Nappa collection;
the silk fabrics are Leontes, colours 1
and 2, from the Perdita collection.
All by Nina Campbell. The platinum
saucer and lilac cup are hand-painted
Limoges, from Nina Campbell's shop.
Right The wallpaper is Eglomise,
colour 4, from the Nappa collection
by Nina Campbell; the paint swatches
are Denim and Popcorn from Nina
Campbell's collection for The Paint
Library. The gold papier-mâché bowl is
from Nina Campbell's shop.

Fabrics and Wallpapers

Metallics and Plains

Reflective surfaces have an important tradition in interior design – the combination of mirror and candlelight, for example, never fails to delight. Over the last few years, it has been wonderful to see wallpaper and fabrics embrace the glamour of metallic finishes, creating an unashamedly luxurious look. When combined with well thought-out lighting, the effect is glorious.

However, if you are to achieve a sophisticated look rather than a tawdry one, it is important not to go too far. The role of plains has always been to provide a neutral foil for the more spectacular ingredients of a scheme. Contrasts are important, so remember that for every glossy surface you introduce, there should also be a matt one to enhance its impact.

Left The bottom fabric swatch is Nappa Plain, colour 13, from the Nappa collection; the paint swatch is Gustave from Nina Campbell's collection for The Paint Library; the two fabric swatches on top are Grosgram, colours 17 and 18, from the Grosgram collection. All fabrics by Nina Campbell. The delphinium hand-painted Limoges plate is from Nina Campbell's shop.

Left *The fabric is Chittagong Stripe, colour 7, from the Chittagong collection by Nina Campbell. The shoe is Nina's own.*

Stripes and Brights

Stripes are an essential tool of the decorator's kit bag, introducing a sense of order and geometry into an interior. Their versatility in terms of colour and pattern means they are as relevant today as they were two hundred years ago or more. As with plains, they are the perfect foil for more elaborate designs.

Whereas most people are happy to use stripes, many shy away from the brights. In fact, you should think of them as the equivalent of spice when cooking: you do not want them to dominate, but simply to add a tang of unexpected flavour. Use them in small amounts and they will be sure to bring a layer of vitality into a room.